Camp Westminster

The Early Years

All profits from the sale of this book
will be donated to Camp Westminster.

ISBN 978-1512332117

Contact the camp at:

Camp Westminster
2412 Lake Rockaway Road
Conyers GA 30012

www.campwestminster.org

Camp Westminster

The Early Years

or

Why I know the streets of Heaven are

paved with Red Georgia clay

Karen Kany King

Paved with Red Georgia Clay (1955)

Contents

My prayer is that this book will cause others to remember their camp experiences and share those memories with friends and family.

Introduction

by Wayne Herring

IN THE SPRING of 1960, my parents informed me
that I would be attending Camp Westminster
in Conyers, Georgia, a ministry of Atlanta's
Westminster Presbyterian Church. They had been
strongly encouraged to do this by J. Julius Scott,
who was our pastor at the Brandon Mississippi
Presbyterian Church. Scott had previously served
as the camp director, beginning at its inception in
1955. I strongly resisted going because I wanted
to concentrate on summer baseball. My parents
prevailed!

Little did I know what a life-changing event this
would be. I was raised as a covenant child and do
not know when I became a Christian. However,
at Camp Westminster, I grew spiritually probably
more than at any other time in my life. For the first
time, I was around serious Christians, both campers and counselors. In addition, I had tons of fun.
I went back for four summers. I met Karen Kany
King, one of several Orlando girls, during her third
summer. We have remained life-long friends and
have often chatted about camp memories.

Karen has done a great job in this little book of
telling what camp life was really like. And through
it, she has done the church of Jesus Christ a big
favor, not only from an historical perspective but

also as an eyewitness report to others. I have been a Presbyterian pastor for over forty years and have no doubt that the foundation I received at Camp Westminster had much to do with my calling into the ministry. Over the decades, I have met literally hundreds of individuals whose lives were affected deeply by spending time at this camp. The testaments continue even to this day.

Thank you, Karen, for putting together thoughts and memories of a special place that God has used to bless the church greatly.

One final note: During my last summer at camp, I met Joyce Horton, the girl who became my wife. Our camp romance made it. We shared 45+ years of a very special marriage.

Wayne Herring   Feb. 19, 2015
Church Relations Officer
Presbyterian Church in America,
    Administrative Committee

Associate Pastor
Covenant Presbyterian Church
Nashville, Tennessee

You Know You Have Arrived (1959)

Foreword

IT IS A hot sunny summer day in mid July and I just went for a walk in my back yard, in New Jersey of all places. There is a big old pine tree back there surrounded by crushed needles, and it has white sap dripping down its side. The smell of that hot pine on a summer day washes over me, bringing tears to my eyes, taking me back more than fifty years ... there we are sitting around the picnic table below the tabernacle, Nancy, Kathy, Wayne, Jimmy, Joey and I, playing a game we made up, "don't blink" ... trying to stare each other down and laughing so hard it became impossible. . . .

But I am jumping ahead. That smell of hot pine brings back waves of memories from the most wonderful and formative summers of my life, the summers I spent at Camp Westminster in Conyers, GA, and it makes me very homesick. I think I have been homesick for camp for over fifty years.

Girls' Cabins (1966)

My First Day at Camp . . .

Turn your eyes upon Jesus
Look full in His wonderful face
And the things of earth will grow strangely dim
in the light of His glory and grace.

DRIVING EAST OUT of Atlanta on a hot early July afternoon, we took the Old Covington Highway to the left turn for Lake Rockaway Road. We followed that for several miles, then turned off the paved road onto red Georgia clay. There was a green and white sign on the right side of the driveway; "We would see Jesus," it boldly claimed. There were tall loblolly pine trees all around us. We drove slowly into the camp grounds, passing the softball field, turning left, and stopping in front of the administration building. There was the strong smell of pine in the hot air.

These were my first moments at Camp Westminster in 1958. I was being sent away to camp for two whole weeks, along with my older brother, and I was very apprehensive. We were part of nearly a hundred other junior high campers from all over the south.

The "Ad" building was long and thin. We entered the lobby, which had large glass windows on two sides, and, I discovered later, was the only place at camp with air conditioning and a cold drinking fountain. Several soft chairs and a white couch were along the walls, above which was a picture of Dr. John R. Richardson, the camp founder. One of the ladies from Westminster Presbyterian Church had made a framed cross-stitching which said "Jesus Christ the same yesterday, today and forever." Doors opening off the lobby led to the counselors' office and director's office which held desks, study books, and the only phone at camp. Beyond the lobby were a craft room, the infirmary, and a guest room.

I found myself, slightly bewildered, standing in front of a long table where new campers were to register. The table was covered with papers, small 3×5 card boxes, pencils, and registration and activity forms. Behind them sat several girl counselors. Knox, the assistant director, a young man with light hair, glasses, and a very thick southern accent stepped forward and said, "Hey, Karen. Welcome to camp. We're glad y'all are here." I looked at him thinking, Who is he and how does he know my name?

I was instructed to fill out an activity form – swimming, archery, softball, crafts ... and assigned to Cabin 5 with India, who wouldn't be at the cabin because she was the lifeguard and at the pool. We drove to an area just above the girls' cabins and unloaded my trunk. Several boys on the work crew were helping carry luggage to the cabins. After picking the bottom bunk, second from the end, and making it up with old lavender sheets, I stuffed my orange flowered Sunday dress along with puffy crinolines into my locker, put on my bathing suit, shoved my trunk under the bed, and headed for the pool to meet my counselor and take my swimming test.

Camp Director Knox Chamblin
(From the 1960 Camp Westminster Brochure)

The pool was brand new that year. The first two years campers had hiked to nearby Lake Rockaway to swim. Now camp had a new Olympic-sized pool surrounded by a large fenced-in patio. There was a turquoise and white diving board at the deep end and a lifeguard chair on the side. The life guard was India, my counselor. She was beautiful, had very fair skin and long auburn red hair which was tied back with a black ribbon matching her black bathing suit. She instructed me in her slow Mississippi drawl to jump in, swim across and back, and tread water. Once I passed the test I was free to swim until time to change for afternoon Bible class with Dr. Richardson. I think we could buy a snack from the candy store which was a shed in a poison ivy patch across from the caretakers' cottage/dining hall/boys' sleeping area. By the next year there was a new dining hall next to the Ad building and several cabins in the boys' area in the woods beyond the pool.

The Original Caretaker's Cottage (1959)

If I remember correctly, Dr. Richardson taught Christian Economics in the afternoon before supper in the tabernacle every day of every camp session every year for the nine summers I was involved with camp. We loved Dr. Richardson but paid little attention in his class. We were tired, hungry, and did not understand the importance of his message. All year the members of Westminster Church in Atlanta collected empty baby food jars. During craft activity every camp session we made banks. These consisted of small wooden trays which held five jars each with a slit cut in the top and a label on the side – "income," "God's money 10%," "others 5%," "saving 5%," and "spending." These illustrated Dr. Richardson's message. As much as we complained, some of us actually learned something. I used the idea of the banks while teaching Vacation Bible School in my home church years later to teach how important it is to tithe. I taught my own children to handle money by making banks with them when they started getting allowance. Wayne told me he used Dr. Richardson's system after he was married in order to live within his budget.

Supper was served family style in the main room of the old caretakers' cottage just beyond the tabernacle that first year. After supper the area had to be cleared and the tables and chairs put away as that was also the boys' sleeping area.

In 1958 five girls' cabins and the pool were new. By the next summer there would be boys' cabins and a new dining hall with living quarters for the cooks in the back, and a second phone for ordering supplies. Over the years the new candy story with guest rooms in the back was built out west beyond the Ad building and parking lot. A new dorm on the road to the lake, built several years later, was often used as two girls' cabins. A guest house/director's house, (later used as the infirmary) was the last new building during my years. The lodge and barn came later.

We had a vespers service in the tabernacle in the evening after supper each night. We sang hymns, learned choruses, read Scripture, and one of the boy counselors preached. It seemed like all summer they were working on and worrying about their sermons. For many years we had an evening activity after dark, "Surprise Hour" the last thing before we went back to our cabins for bed. This could be anything like an evening swim – often the director or one of the counselors got pushed in with his clothes on. A treasure hunt was wild excitement finding frogs with flashlights, cutting counselors' toe nails, or stealing love letters. Most fun were counselor hunts during which all the counselors hid someplace on the camp grounds and the campers, divided into four teams, had to find them and touch them to win team points. Counselors were often found in a canoe on the lake, on a roof, up a tree, or in a blackberry thicket. The blackberry thicket was my favorite spot as a junior and senior counselor. I remember hiding there with Laura one summer and eating all the berries. The winning team was rewarded with a watermelon. After a number of years, sometime in the early 60s, this schedule was switched, Surprise Hour was right after supper and the more serious evening vespers came right before bedtime. Many of us did not like the change! We liked the activities in the dark.

Cabin Area

Out of the ivory palaces
Into a world of woe,
Only His great eternal love
Made my Savior go.

That He should leave His place on high
And come for sinful man to die,
You count it strange? So once did I,
Before I knew my Savior.

CABIN 5 WAS my home away from home for many summers. India then Laura and later Kathy were my counselors there. One summer we campers who were friends were separated and spread out into other cabins in order to make new friends, which we did not like. I was the counselor in Cabin 1 (which had always been "mother Murray's" cabin and later Lisa's) during my last two summers at camp when I was a senior counselor myself. As much as I loved Cabin 1, I still missed Cabin 5.

That first year I became friends with some of the girls in my cabin. Pam and I used to study together for Bible quizzes. We would spend rest time, after lunch, and much of our time at the pool memorizing large parts of scripture and asking each other detailed questions. Once I was very angry when

Knox said my answer was wrong; I knew I had been right and Pam came to my defense. Bible quizzes pitted five members of each cabin against another cabin team of five in a round robin that went on the whole camp session. We would sit on the stage in the tabernacle in two rows of five chairs. Knox usually was in charge. He would read the question and the first camper on his or her feet would have a chance to answer. Other counselors sat in the audience with the campers and judged who was on his or her feet first. Points were given for each correct answer. Many answers included memorized verses.

We all loved to sing. Some of us used to help each other learn to sing parts. I remember being thrilled to learn alto for one of my favorite hymns . . . "Out of the Ivory Palaces, into a world of woe, only His great eternal love, made my Savior go". I can hear the alto in my head as I write!

We worked hard to keep our cabin clean. After breakfast each morning was cabin cleanup time. Campers spent about twenty minutes cleaning their cabins. One person would "police the area" getting every candy wrapper, piece of lint, and stick out of the area around the cabin. Wet towels had to be perfectly straight on the line. Inside campers would make beds, all corners had to be square and sheets tight; sweep and dust, every "woolie" had to be found and removed; and all clothes and personal belongings had to be put into lockers and trunks and suitcases. One year one of the girls brought a toy stuffed octopus with braided legs, each with a different colored ribbon on the end, which she kept on her bunk. We got points taken off one morning because all eight legs were not even and straight. There were long rivalries between some of the cabins. Some cabins, like Cabin 6, had their own songs . . . "Tough as nails, hard as bricks, we're the girls from cabin six". The campers with the cleanest cabin all camp session got a watermelon all to themselves on the last day which was eaten on the picnic table by the dining hall in front of everyone.

The Woods Outside Cabin 1 (1966)

One friend I remember was Johnnie from South Carolina. She had dark hair and freckles and was very funny. She helped write our play for skit night and then hurt her leg and ended up in the infirmary so she could not be in the skit. We were heartbroken. Nancy, Kathy and I spent many hours visiting her in the back room of the Ad building before she returned to the cabin. In the cabin at night we had evening devotions led by the junior counselor. At the end of the evening devotions we took turns saying prayers. Johnnie's prayers were always refreshing to listen to, she just talked to God. One night after she said "amen" there was a long silence and then she said "PS" and added more to her prayer. We all giggled then but I never forgot how sincerely she talked to God who was right there with her.

On Sunday afternoon during rest hour after lunch we had to write home to our parents. Since camp was two weeks long we had to let them know we were still alive. On other days during that time we slept, read, studied for Bible quizzes, wrote letters to friends, or talked quietly.

Before lunch, after morning activities, we would gather on our cabin porch for Bible study. I remember being taught as a camper and later, as a counselor, teaching both Romans and Hebrews. I can still see India in her black bathing suit sitting on a chair tilted back against the porch post explaining the difference between God's perfect and permissive will, speaking in her slow Mississippi accent. She explained that, as Romans 8 states, God has predestined us to be exactly what/who He wants us to be as we follow Him. But because He gave us free will we sometimes make our own choices and do not follow His perfect will, we stray off the path He has chosen for us. By loving us and disciplining us He brings us back to His will after we have taken the long way around; that is His permissive will. That was a very reassuring lesson.

About seven years later, when I was the counselor in Cabin 1, I had the responsibility of teaching similar Bible lessons to my ten girls each session. My junior high girls that summer were especially bright and creative. They played many fun pranks, but usually listened attentively and asked good questions during our Bible study time.

Near the end of the first week of the session a number of "care packages" from home had arrived. These were fought over, hidden, stolen, but mostly shared. One such package had arrived the day before containing Oreo cookies. I was trying to teach the lesson that hot July morning just before lunch. We were all sitting on the cement porch, some on chairs or pillows or towels. My girls were more interested in whispering and eating cookies than listening. Finally, as they were all giggling, and looking behind where they were sitting, I asked what was so much more important than my lesson. I soon found out. God's lesson was far more important!

One of the girls had dropped her Oreo on the porch near the corner. Very quickly a line of ants came marching from the cabin yard, up the side of the cement, across the corner of the porch, *up* and *over* the Oreo cookie, continuing on their way off the porch and on into the woods. The girls were laughing because the ants were so stupid, they walked right over the huge cookie and kept going. There was enough food there in that one cookie to feed their whole nest for days or even weeks and they didn't see it! One girl had tried to stop the ants but they kept marching in a line right over her finger. Another girl tried to pick one up and send it back to the cookie. I stopped trying to teach the lesson and joined the girls.

We began a very involved discussion about how we could make the ants realize the huge food source in front of them. It would solve all their problems. We tried rerouting the ants, moving the cookie, breaking the cookie, separating the chocolate cookie from the white filling, explaining the situation to the ants, yelling at the ants . . . nothing worked. They just kept blindly marching on their own way. Anyone watching our cabin would have thought we were nuts!

"What if we could speak ant language, then we could tell them about the cookie being a huge food supply", one girl said. Another girl explained that wouldn't help because we are too big and loud. If we started talking to them it would be like a voice from heaven scaring them. "What if one of us could become an ant and go up to them with our little feelers (with her fingers on the sides of head wiggling) touching their feelers, telling them about the cookie?", said one of the more quiet thoughtful girls. We finally decided that would be the only way to communicate with the stupid one-track-minded ants.

We are just like ants, I pointed out to the girls. We go our own way paying no attention to the riches of eternal life God has set before us. He has tried telling us many times and in many different ways but we didn't understand, just as it says in the beginning of Hebrews. Finally God the Son became the man Jesus, spoke people language, and told us how we can have life, enough for eternity. He did for us what we can never do for ourselves, gave His life in order to make eternal life available to us. Several girls listened to what God said to them in their own language that session and accepted Jesus as God Himself who came to save them.

The story about the ants became part of camp lore and has been used many times over the years since that hot July day, in other camp sessions, Sunday school, VBS, Bible study groups, and sermons. About forty years later I even heard Steve Brown on the radio on Key Life tell a very similar story and wondered where he had heard it . . .

In the center of the girls' cabin area was the bath house. There were three stalls (three more added years later) one very long sink with several faucets and an open shower area with three shower heads. We dreaded taking showers in ice cold spring water, and assumed we were clean from swimming in the chlorine water of the pool. Once a week on Saturday we HAD to take a shower. The most dangerous part of showering was shampooing one's hair. In those days all shampoo bottles were glass and often the bottle would slip and the cement shower floor would be covered with a combination of slippery soap and pieces of glass. We all started using Prell when it was the first brand to sell shampoo in a bright green plastic toothpaste-shaped tube. Oh, the smell of Prell!!! Because we hated the cold showers (hot water was added years later) three or four of us at a time would stand at the long sink with one foot up in the sink shaving our legs. That was a funny sight.

The "johns" did not always work well and the boys on the work crew hated coming to fix our toilets. One year while we waited for the work crew to arrive, Ethel, one of the junior counselors whom we all loved because she was quiet, very beautiful, and sweet, just walked in and "fixed" the toilet with her bare hands. We thought she was even more amazing when she just shrugged and said, "it needed to be done." She taught me the lesson that a true friend is one who is willing to help "clean the toilet" of another person's life, with a smile, because it needs to be done.

The only stories I ever heard about the boys' bath house had to do with boys who were unruly being stung with "rat tails," wet towels that were rolled up so there is a point at one end that are popped against another person's skin, which, I understand, really stings.

One summer the mother of one the boy campers would very often just show up at camp, checking on her son. His counselor, Steve, was very bothered by this. One afternoon Steve looked out of the bath house and saw this mother standing in the boys' cabin area. With no clothes on he put only his towel around his head so no one would recognize him and walked from the bath house to the cabin. That mother never showed up unannounced again!

From the 1960 Camp Westminster Brochure

Pranks

Blest be the tie that binds
Our hearts in Christian love;
The fellowship of kindred minds
is like to that above.

WE HAD SO much fun playing pranks. Something new and different would happen every summer. Very soon after I arrived the first summer, India pointed out a small brown suitcase which had initials on it sitting in our cabin as we were going to bed. She told us it belonged to a new camper whose luggage was sent to camp before she arrived. I don't remember how she convinced us not to tell anyone.

The next morning at breakfast, Benny, one of the boy counselors, arrived in borrowed clothes that were too small, probably Knox's. Benny's suitcase was hidden in our cabin. So much for our new camper! I think that was one of the many mornings men's underwear was up the flag pole.

Speaking of underwear, the small tree outside Cabin 1 was decorated with all my underwear one bright summer day, just like a Christmas Tree. It gave new meaning to "Christmas in July."

In the early 1960s we girls wore split skirts under which we wore pantaloons or a split slip. I had a pair of pantaloons that had several layers of eyelet with little blue ribbons running through each layer as well as lace on the bottom edge. Those pantaloons were in my laundry bag one break when several of the boys on the work crew volunteered to take the counselors' laundry into Conyers to the laundromat. Later that afternoon when I was walking toward the Ad building, Wayne and Jimmy were watching me. When I opened the door there were my pantaloons heavily starched and ironed and standing by themselves in the middle of the lobby.

When I was a counselor I told my girls that pranks were fine as long as they didn't hurt anyone or destroy property; that was one way to ensure creativity. One year the junior high girls put Glad Wrap stretched tightly over the toilet, then put the seat down . . . Later they put "poppers" (little pressure fire crackers that pop when thrown on the sidewalk) between the toilet seat and the rim of the toilet. We all learned to check carefully before using the bath house.

One boys' cabin, hoping to be very clean, stacked all the bunks like a pyramid so there was more open floor and it would be easier to sweep. One night the poor boy on the top bunk had his big toe stuck into the socket from which the bulb had been taken, then the switch was turned on. That was a shocking way to wake up!!!

There was a small four-drawer dresser in each cabin for the counselor. Returning from the pool to my cabin to get dressed for the evening, I opened my top dresser drawer. There were my shorts instead of my underwear. I calmly took out what I wanted to wear and opened the next drawer where I found my underwear instead of shirts, and the last drawer from which I took a shirt. My back was to the campers but I could hear muffled comments. I had disappointed them by not being upset to find all my drawers rearranged, and acting like life was normal. I never put the drawers back in the right order. The next day my junior counselor Linda and I returned to find our whole bunk bed on the front porch where we happily slept each night for the rest of the summer!!! It was fun frustrating pranksters by not responding to the pranks.

Cabin 1's Front Porch, My "Home," Summer 1966

Counselors played pranks on the campers, too. One rainy night in Cabin 5, Laura went outside to make sure the canvas tarps were down to keep out the rain. She started making noise like a wild bobtail cat prowling around. She got another counselor, I think it was Helen, to come down and inspect the area and they were "sure" they found wildcat footprints in the mud. Another night several of the boy counselors cut large green teeth from watermelon rind, covered their faces with shaving cream and black watermelon seeds, and turned on flashlights from their chins up. They "haunted" both the boys' and girls' cabin areas.

Jack Allen was one of the boy counselors during my last summer at camp. He had driven his VW bug from his home in Yazoo Mississippi to camp that summer. He loved that car and took very good care of it. He was not inclined to let other counselors use it. One fine afternoon after Jack returned to camp, probably from an errand to Conyers, he left it parked outside the dining hall. The keys were in it!!! It took me quite a long time but after many trips to the back of the craft room in the Ad building I totally stuffed his car with wadded up newspaper, locked the car, and hid the key. I left a little note on the door which was the beginning clue of a treasure hunt . . . each clue led to another somewhere on the camp grounds. The last clue told where to locate the key. I think it took him about a week to discover that the picture of Knox in the Ad building lobby was holding the key. I had wanted to drive the car through the dining hall doors and leave it in back of the tables, but Charles talked me out of that as it would have left an oil mark on the tile. That building now has a cement floor. The old tile is all gone and the building is to be replaced soon.

Between the two-week camp sessions we had a "free" weekend. Sometimes counselors would leave camp and visit friends, go home, or go away and visit a boyfriend and become engaged, which I did during my last summer. Often we would organize a group activity for the counselors staying at camp. These usually had to do with food. One break we all went to get pizza. The evening ended up being an all-you-can-eat contest. I ate a whole "everything" pizza myself!!! Another evening we went to Mammy's Shanty, a very nice restaurant near Five Points in Atlanta. We girls got dressed up, which included wearing stockings and a girdle back then, even if we didn't need a girdle. Half way through the meal Nancy, Kathy and I went to the ladies' room and took off our girdles and stuffed them in our pocket books because we had eaten way, way too much.

Picture from an Atlanta Newspaper, 1959

Creatures

Praise God, from whom all blessings flow;
Praise Him all creatures here below;
Praise Him above, ye heavenly host;
Praise Father, Son, and Holy Ghost.

BECAUSE CAMP IS in the middle of a pine woods on over a hundred acres with a lake, humans weren't the only ones who attended camp.

Some of the creatures were very tame. During my last summer at camp in 1966, Charles the director and his family lived in the guest house with their little white toy poodle. He used to play in the yard keeping baby John company.

Sometimes during the weekend break, staff who had worked at the camp previous summers would take newer counselors "snipe hunting." There was an elaborate ritual including flashlights and bags to capture the snipes. None were ever caught, the new counselors felt foolish, and I believed for years that there was no such thing as a snipe. My husband, who is quite a serious birder, tells me there is truly a snipe.

A more productive activity during break time was frog gigging. Three or four of us would get frog gigs, flashlights, and big black garbage bags and slowly paddle along the edge of the lake at night in one of the canoes shining our lights looking for frog eyes. One summer the cooks told us that if we caught the frogs they would cook frog legs for us. Several of the junior staff and work crew including me, Wayne and I think Jimmy and Joey, spent most of a night out on the lake. We gigged at least a dozen large frogs. We dragged the bag of frogs up to the dining hall and left them in the walk-in freezer.

The cooks were away for the weekend. When they returned the frogs were a frozen mass which could not be used. They should have been cleaned before they were frozen. What a waste of good frog legs, but what fun we had! Was that the night we got shut in the freezer and had to wait for someone to come rescue us?

The senior girl counselors would get up early in the morning before the campers and go down to the pool area, still wearing pj's and curlers, to have devotions together and discuss any problems we had in the cabin area. Mary would come by and quietly tap each of us to wake us up without waking the campers. One morning we discovered a little star-nosed mole swimming around the pool. He was very cute and exhausted. We had no idea how long he had been in there treading water. I fished him out with the long handled net and let him go. He rushed off toward the lake area to find his family I am sure.

One morning Laurie, the boy counselor who was the other lifeguard came down to the pool early to test the Ph of the water. I think he was more embarrassed finding us all there in pj's and curlers than we were.

Not all the creatures were as harmless as puppies, frogs, and moles. One night there was a horrible scream from Cabin 3. Virginia, the head girls' counselor, and most of the other counselors headed in that direction. Virginia was the most brave one of us and extricated a huge furry spider from the rafters. It took quite a while to calm down the girls' cabin area that night.

There were snakes at camp. We were told that if you didn't bother them they wouldn't bother you. I remember seeing a big black one swimming in the lake one night. What must have been about my third summer at camp Nancy and I arrived only to find ALL the trees and undergrowth around the girls' area, especially Cabin 5, gone! We were so upset. That is what had made the area secluded and beautiful. Knox had had it bulldozed down so India would be less frightened.

India was back from the hospital in time to be our counselor that camp session. As she told the story, she had been praying for patience for some time. One day earlier in the summer after lunch as she started back to the girls' cabins from the dining hall she saw a copperhead snake in the middle of the road. She didn't want the girls to go near it but they were supposed to return to the cabin for rest period. So India picked up a rock and threw it at the snake which was several yards away. She was trying to frighten it away. When it didn't move she threw a second rock. As she reached for a third rock on the ground the snake sprung at her, not from a coiled position, and bit her on the hand. Knox heard the commotion, came out of the Ad building and administered first aid by sucking the venom out of the wound. One of the boy counselors who was in the Ad building at the same time happened to have read, over the weekend about what to do in a snake bite emergency and remembering the phone number from the article called for help. India ended up in the hospital for several days being treated for the snake bite. She told us the worst part was having to remain quiet and physically still for a long time. That experience she told us, really taught her patience. She warned us campers, who were all serious new Christians, to be careful what we pray for because God will probably answer our prayers in ways we would never expect, like a snake bite to teach her patience!

There are stories of some of the boys catching snakes and bringing them into the cabin with a rope around the neck for a leash. I can't imagine that ever happened in the girls' cabin area.

The only other "vicious creatures" at camp were chiggers. Chiggers are little microscopic bugs that get under your skin and itch like crazy. They usually bite where clothing is tightest against the body. We girls often had chigger bites anywhere we were touched by our underwear. The best way to kill the little buggers was to suffocate them and the best way to do that was to paint the spots on the skin where they lived with fingernail polish. Many of us spent the summer with pink painted spots in unmentionable places.

Speaking of itching; many areas of camp had

large patches of poison ivy. There was one such patch across from the old caretaker's house by the shed that had functioned as the candy store for the first few years of camp.

One day, my very first summer, as we were waiting in line to buy treats, one of the boys bragged that he could not get poison ivy. Of course another boy dared him to touch the leaves in the very large patch behind the candy store. He marched right in, took his shirt off, lay down, and rolled around in the leaves. The rest of the session he was not a happy camper!

That was when I learned how to recognize the three shiny leaves of poison ivy!

Camper Counselor Time (1959)
with Future Camp Directors

Lessons

Summer and winter, and springtime and harvest,
Sun, moon and stars in their courses above,
Join with all nature in manifold witness
To Thy great faithfulness, mercy and love.

THERE WERE TWO sides to camp like two sides of
a coin. There were the many and varied fun activities, and there were the serious theological lessons.
Somehow these were held together by the growing
friendships between campers and counselors.

My first lesson was personal and made me realize
there is no such thing as a coincidence. A number
of random things happened the first week that suddenly came together. The very first day of camp
Knox had greeted me by name. I was curious how
he knew my name and impressed at the same time.
Out of all the people at camp how did he know my
name? During the first few nights at camp Kathy,
Pam and I had sneaked out and just walked around
looking up at the immense starry sky. Sometimes
we sat on the huge rock on the way to the boys'
cabin area next to the tree that had been struck by
lightning years before. It was beautiful, scary, and
made me feel so small. One of the boys, Jimmy,
had told me how you are supposed to ask Jesus
for forgiveness for your sins and ask him into your

heart. That sounded strange to me . . . I wasn't sure about the sin part . . . did that mean sins against me, too? Near the end of the first week Benny, one of the boy counselors, spoke at vespers. He pointed out that in the huge universe, created by God, the earth is just a tiny speck. And, on that tiny speck are even smaller specks, people. Yet each tiny speck of a person is so important to God that He knows and loves us individually. He even knows your individual personal name! He loves you so much He sent His Son to make you His own child.

A few nights later that July I suddenly woke up and sat up in my bunk, the next to the last bunk on the bottom in Cabin 5, while everyone else was asleep. I stared out into the woods. I know there wasn't an audible voice, but I heard God call me by name and ask me to give myself to Him. I knew beyond any doubt that I was loved, cleansed, valued and saved. It was not a frightening experience but extremely reassuring. My life has never been the same!!!

Without that experience I would never have understood all the lessons I learned over the many summers at camp. Some were simple lessons using words like "sin." It is "sin" because "I" am right in the middle. "JOY" means Jesus first, others second and yourself last. My favorite was "atonement" which means we are meant to be at one with God . . . "at-one-ment." And to be "justified" means, I am now loved by God just-if-I'd never sinned.

We campers often shared our own ideas and insights with each other. It was from a camper that

I realized God values and uses us even if we are different. A short person can be "ten feet tall in God's eyes" if he allows himself to be used by God for His glory.

One day Sandy, a missionary kid from Brazil, and I were standing on the hill between the girls' cabin area and the pool. He was telling me the way he understands the Trinity. While growing up in Brazil he and his brothers and sister were pretty isolated. His mother had a room in their house which was the school room where she taught them every morning. In the afternoon she organized games and activities for them to play. And, in the evening, she made supper and tucked them in bed. She was their Teacher, Friend, and Mother, yet always the same one person.

One very hot day, after I had attended camp for several years, a group of us were down by the lake during afternoon swim time. During those times when we were just goofing around "wasting time" we were really having serious conversations. We were siting on the picnic table taking turns scratching each other's backs. Charles started telling us about a dream he had had the night before about a wedding in Heaven. We began to discuss how the dream was like Revelation and wondered what heaven must be like. That discussion made heaven very real to me. I remembered that conversation about eight years later after Nance was tragically killed in a car accident . . . she is in a very real place. (Nancy and I had grown up in the same church in Orlando. Starting in seventh grade we were in the same junior high school and became very close "best" friends. I talked her into going to camp with me for what would be my third summer. Although she never became a counselor as I did, we attended camp together every summer until our senior year in high school. Her family moved to Atlanta the summer before our senior year. She was very sad and wanted to finish high school in Orlando. I was jealous that she was moving "right next door" to camp! During the next few years she drove out to camp many evenings for vespers and stayed to visit. She was in my wedding the Christmas after my last summer at camp. She was married the following Thanksgiving and was tragically killed the next day in a car accident on a wet rainy highway. Years later, when my "Mama" died, Nancy's mother came to Orlando to the funeral. She gave me a big hug and said, "I wonder if your Mama and Nancy have talked to each other and caught up on all the news yet." That is how real heaven is!!!)

Once in a while we would have an outside speaker in the evening. I remember Dr. Richardson introducing a good friend who was Jewish. He spoke about the Jews in the OT and the Jewish traditions he had followed as a boy growing up. He told us how he had finally realized one day that Jesus is the Messiah who was prophesied in the OT. I remember him saying very seriously that as a Christian he was very proud to be a Jew because Jesus was a Jew. Ever since that night I have had great respect for Jews.

One of the boy counselors, I think it was Cobby,

who loved to play golf, told us that he knew then-President Eisenhower. When asked about it he said he played golf on the same course near his home in Georgia where the president played. One day he was with a group of players who were just behind the group with whom the president was playing. Then Cobby was asked when he met the president and what he said. He had to admit that he had never actually "met" the president but knew all about him and played golf on the same course.

We often know all about God and attend church where He can be found but never actually personally meet Him. We can't say we know God unless we meet Him personally and have a relationship with Him.

(From the 1960 Camp Westminster Brochure)

Talks

I love to tell the story, Tis pleasant to repeat
What seems, each time I tell it, More wonderfully
sweet,
I love to tell the story, For some have never heard
The message of salvation from God's own Holy
Word.

THERE ARE SEVERAL talks that stand out in my mind after all these years. They illustrate what it is to understand God's love for each individual through Christ's work.

I don't remember which of the boy counselors spoke . . . Cobby?

THE KING AND HIS THREE SONS

THERE WAS AN old king of a vast kingdom who was kind and good and wise. The king was getting old and needed a plan to care for the subjects he loved after his death. He had tried to teach his three sons to be good, kind, and wise like he was. He called his three sons to him. He set up a test for them, the one who was wise enough to pass the test would inherit all his wealth, his whole vast kingdom, and have the responsibility to care for and love his subjects. He took them out to the old huge barn beyond the back field to the east of the castle. They quietly walked inside the vast empty space with the lingering smells of horses, hay and roosting chickens. "The son who completely fills this old barn with just ONE thing will inherit all," he said. He turned to the oldest son and told him he would be first and he had one month to complete the task, then walked away leaving the boys to think.

The oldest son was proud to be chosen first. He wanted his father's wealth and he wanted it soon. He could think of many ways to spend the money and the grand lifestyle he would have. He announced to the other brothers that he already had a perfect plan and he would begin the next day.

First thing in the morning he called all the servants and began ordering them around, yelling at them and even kicking them if they didn't hurry. Finally after weeks of trucks coming and going, the smell of tar, and large scaffolding on the north side of the barn with seats on top, and scraps of plastic everywhere, he called his father and brothers. Cocky, believing that he would soon be wealthy and famous, he escorted his family up to the seats on top of the scaffolding. As they sat there looking down into the vast empty space through a crack between the wall and roof, the eldest son began pumping water from the lake into the old barn now lined with plastic and sealed with pitch. Soon it would be full and he would win his father's favor. The second brother began to whine and complain that he would be left out. The youngest son just quietly watched.

The water rose and they heard squeaks and groans as the pressure built on the old wooden building. Suddenly the little chicken door on the south side leading out to the chicken yard burst under the pressure and the water began to rush out faster than it was pumped in. The second brother gloated and said he now had a chance to win all the father's wealth.

The second son, who was angry that he was never first, vowed he would win in the wake of his big brother's failure. The king also gave him one month to complete the task of filling the barn with just one thing to try to prove he was as wise as his father.

He taunted the older brother for being so stupid and told the youngest brother he's never have a chance. The younger brother didn't seem to mind. He went out every day to help his father care of the subjects in the kingdom. This made the second brother even more angry and he tried to find out what ideas the younger brother had to fill the barn. The youngest brother just smiled and said he would wait his turn.

For three weeks chicken dinners were cooked every night for the whole family by the wife of the second son. Large flat bed trucks brought in several motors which he mounted in the windows and wires which all lay in a big tangle around the barn ended in one long cord stretched all the way to the castle.

At last the second son stomped into the room and demanded they all come to the barn. He had them stand in one corner as he gave the signal to his servant by the castle to plug in the cord. The motors began running fans which blew on baskets of feathers left from all those chicken dinners, so that they blew up into the air and seemingly filled the barn . . . until the second son's prized pig ran by outside and tripped over the cord unplugging it causing the feathers to fall into a one foot layer on the floor of the barn.

The second son swore and kicked at the feathers as if he could make them fly again before stomping out of the barn a failure.

The king turned to his youngest son and said because he was younger and had less experience he would give him two months to prove his wisdom by filling the barn with just one thing. He humbly told his father he didn't need that long. Then he quietly asked his family to meet him in the barn the next night at midnight.

He spent the next day cleaning up the mess the older brother had made, and repairing the old barn. Just before midnight the family followed the now familiar path from the castle to the old barn under a moonless overcast sky.

The youngest son silently seated them in comfortable chairs he had brought from the castle that had been placed around a small table. He then lit a candle and placed it on the table. Light filled the vast empty barn and even spilled out into the barnyard through cracks in the old walls.

This son received all that was his father's.

Light exposes defects and reveals Truth. Without

God your life is as empty and dark as the first two sons. You try to fill your life with material things but find that they always fall short of making your life complete. Only by putting Christ at the center of your life can that emptiness be filled and your darkness made light. Jesus said he came as the light of the world and whoever believed in Him would not live in darkness.

SAD FATHER AND SON

I believe it was Charles who used this illustration during one of his evening talks.

THERE WAS A wealthy young man who had inherited his family's property and business. He was kind, a man of integrity, honest and very good at his business. He became very wealthy and used much of his wealth to better the lives of others.

One day he fell deeply in love with a beautiful, loving, kind young women. They traveled around the world for a year for their honeymoon. They bought expensive souvenirs from around the world with which to decorate their home, met famous national leaders, and became involved in a number of charity organizations especially in third world countries.

Several years after they returned home and settled down they had a baby boy. Although they lived in a large beautiful home with many expensive belongings, furniture, cars, boats, clothes . . . they did not spoil their son, but taught him to love and care for others.

When their son was born, they hired a house-keeper/nurse to help care for the baby. She was carefully screened to make sure she would teach him their same values of love and responsibility. There were others in the household, the butler, driver, gardener, cook, and maid, but he was especially close to the housekeeper.

When the boy was about three, his mother became very ill and died. The young father was devastated. Everything in the house reminded him of his lovely wife, especially his young son whose eyes looked so much like hers. The father fell deeper and deeper into grief and finally announced he was going on a long trip. He left the young boy in the care of the housekeeper along with the others who worked for him.

After traveling around the world, stopping in many of the places he and his wife had visited on their honeymoon, the father returned. Over the years while he was away he had learned not to look back in grief but ahead with joy.

When he finally reached home he was very excited to spend time with his son. They played catch, went sailing, backpacking, and mountain climbing. They grew to deeply love and respect each other. They spent hours reading together, discussing politics and religion. The father began teaching his son, age ten, about the family business, how to handle finances, and especially how to help others.

The father threw a big party for his son on his sixteenth birthday. All his friends were invited. They talked, played music, ate, swam and played games long into the night. The next morning at breakfast the father told his son he had a birthday gift for him. He led his son to the back yard behind the hedge and there was a bright red MG convertible with his son's name on the license plate. The son's jaw dropped as the father handed him the keys telling him to take it for a spin around the block.

Minutes later, back at the breakfast table the father could hear a horrible screech and crash followed by sirens not far away. With his heart in his throat the father ran to the next block. He didn't even see the police arresting the driver of the dump truck with the smashed front end. He fell on his knees on the pavement beside his dying son. When the boy died two days later the father felt as if his own life had ended.

The years passed slowly in a dark daze as the father continued his own grief-stricken existence until one day he died of a heart attack . . . some say of a broken heart.

About a week after the father's death his long time friend and lawyer called the household staff into the library to read the will. There was no other family and what didn't go to them would go to charity. The lawyer explained that they could each pick one thing, just one, whatever he or she wanted from the whole estate.

The butler spent the whole afternoon walking around the house trying to make up his mind. He wandered in to the father's room remembering all the pleasant conversations and down the stairs into the music room and living room leaning on the mantle over the big fireplace looking up at the picture of the handsome son. At last he walked into the library where he had spent his leisure hours. I'll take the collection of books, he told the lawyer. He wasn't sure if that was acceptable as there were many rare, first editions, and books from all over the world signed by very important people. The lawyer made arrangements right away to have them packed up for the butler.

The driver acted as if he needed time to think, walking all around the house and grounds but he ended his tour in the second garage stating he wanted the Bentley. The lawyer handed him the title and keys.

The gardener, who had always loved the out of doors and had kept the grounds immaculate, asked for the twenty-acre plot down by the river at the back edge of the property that had never been tilled. The lawyer gave him the deed along with the tractor and tools.

The cook, who had lovingly cooked and served so many meals for the family, could not imagine any other life. After much thought she asked for the dining room table that had been hand made by an Amish craftsman as a wedding gift so many years before. The lawyer gave her the whole dining room set, table, chairs, buffet and china closet along with all the well-used and well-loved cook books.

The maid, who had not lived there as many years as the others, had always loved the huge hand-carved German grandfather clock which stood in the hall at the bottom of the stairs. Its chimes, which filled the house with music, had kept her on schedule while she worked.

Only the housekeeper was left. She had loved and served the father, mother, and son as if they were her own family. How could she leave? How could she choose just one thing? The lawyer encouraged her to take her time. She thought about all the jewelry upstairs and fine clothes. She walked from room to room feeling the valuable oriental rugs under her feet and touching beautiful furniture, some from many countries of the world. She touched the fine china and silver she had helped polish. She sat in the living room with its beautiful antiques thinking of the yacht at the shore and the other cars in the garage. None of those meant anything to her without the family. Where would she go? What would she do? She almost asked those questions aloud as she looked through tears at the handsome picture of the son over the fireplace. At last she turned to the lawyer and explained that the love in the house was what made it special. She said she wanted the portrait of the son who was so loved and had learned to love others.

As the lawyer took it off the wall they discovered an envelope attached to the back of the picture. Inside was a note written and signed by the father, "the one who chooses my son will inherit all that I have".

Although the world and entire universe belongs to God because He created it all, His love and life itself are His greatest possessions. We are asked to choose what we want most. The one who chooses God's Son will inherit all that is His!

Boy and His Boat

I think this story was told by Cobby but I am not sure.

THERE WAS A little boy who wanted a boat to sail on the nearby river. He talked to his Dad and got all the material and directions he needed. He worked very hard and put in long hours on many weekends, when he was not in school, to make the perfect little sailboat with his initial on the top.

Finally it was finished. The white sail was sewn perfectly to the mast. The top surface was painted a gleaming white while the bottom was red. He knew every part of his little boat as he had made it himself just the way he wanted it.

He put a little eye hook in the back where he attached a long string. This way the little boat could sail on its own but not get too far away.

He was all excited when the day came to launch the boat. He took it to the river. The sun was shining, there were flowers on the banks along the river and there was a slight breeze . . . perfect. Day after day he came to the river to sail his little boat.

One day while he was sailing his little boat a strong wind came up. The clouds darkened the sky and the rain began to fall. There was thunder and lightning. His little boat was way out at the end of his long string. As he began to pull it in a small speed boat, driven by a man frightened by the storm, came speeding by headed for the big boat house.

The little boy continued to pull on his boat but suddenly he realized there was nothing at the end of the string. He ran up and down the river edge looking and asking other people about his boat, but it was gone.

Sadly he went home. He didn't even notice he was cold and wet. For many days he returned to the river's edge hoping his little boat might have been blown ashore. Even after cold weather came and ice began to form on the river, he kept returning.

One day his father, wanting to cheer him up, asked if he wanted to go to town with him the next Saturday. While his father attended to his business the boy wandered down the street looking in the store windows.

Suddenly he stopped in front of an old toy store. "New and used toys" the sign said. He went in to look around and there on a shelf behind the cash register was HIS boat. He was sure! "Hey, mister, that's my boat," he said. The man smiled and said, "only after you pay for it." The boy tried to explain what had happened. How he recognized the boat because he had made it. His initial was on the now dirty surface. "You should have seen how bright the white and red were when I painted it," he said.

The store owner said he could have it and quoted a very large sum of money. The boy's face fell. "I'll buy it," he said. "Please hold it for me until I get the money." "I can't hold it forever," the store owner replied.

The boy went home and counted all the money in his bank. He knew before he counted it that it wouldn't be enough. He asked for money for both his birthday and Christmas. He did errands for his parents and neighbors, raked leaves, shoveled snow, cleaned gutters . . . anything.

Finally, as he counted his money one evening he realized he had enough. He ran to his father and asked him to please take him back to the toy store.

When he approached the counter, his heart sank. The boat was no longer on the shelf. He turned to the store owner and asked about it. "I put it down here to hold it for you," he said as he lifted it up to the counter. With great joy the boy emptied his bank onto the counter, all he had. And holding the boat lovingly in his hands he said, "Now you are mine, really mine, twice mine. I made you with great care and I bought you back at a great price."

God made each of us in His own image. We have strayed from Him by our own choice, but He has bought us each back with a great price, the life of His own Son. When we realize this we are His, cherished and loved, really His forever.

Slave Girl

ONE OF THE most powerful stories used at a vespers service was the story of a slave girl. This story is especially important because it shows that

Christ's sacrifice frees people not only from their own sinful nature, but also frees them from sins committed against them by others. Understanding this can allow women/girls who have been abused to realize that they have great value in God's eyes.

BEFORE THE CIVIL WAR a young man traveled many miles to visit his cousin. This young man had inherited his family's fortune and was looking for advice about investing his wealth. They got into a heated discussion about slavery one evening after the cousin invited the young man to accompany him to the slave market the following morning. The young man tried to point out all that was wrong with slavery while his cousin, a plantation owner, explained its necessity.

Early the next morning the cousin rode off to town. Later, driven by curiosity, the young man saddled his horse and followed the road his cousin had taken to town. The young man tied his horse near a tavern and followed the noise of the crowd to the slave market. It was a large white building with a raised porch which had a roof held up by six pillars. Large rings were embedded in each pillar to which slaves were attached while being sold.

Most slaves were scared, sullen and silent. Men who wanted to buy a particular slave would walk up the steps and examine the slave, checking each for diseases, much like one would examine a horse. The auctioneer would point out positive attributes of each slave and name a starting price before the auction began.

The cousin noticed his guest, the young man, in the crowd as he turned to go down the steps after checking one of the strong field hands. He walked over to him and asked if he had changed his mind and wanted to buy a slave after all. The young man said his curiosity had turned to disgust!

The last slave was a young woman who was strong, calm, and poised despite crude remarks made by some men in the crowd. A high price was announced by the auctioneer. Most of the men could not afford to buy her but were curious to see what would happen. A number of wealthy plantation owners began to bid. Finally the bidding was narrowed down to just two men. At that point the young man visiting his cousin stepped forward with a much higher bid. With a sneer his cousin pointed out that he was a hypocrite. The young man gave his cousin a stare as cold as steel and bid even higher. In the end he spent his great wealth, his entire inheritance, to buy the young woman. The crowd cheered as the auctioneer unhooked her from the pillar and pushed her down the steps to the feet of her new owner.

Then the crowd went silent as the young man leaned down and unfastened her shackles. He gently helped her to her feet and, taking off his own coat, placed it around her. He looked directly at her, spoke her name, and said, "I bought you to set you free".

With tears of gratitude in her eyes she fell at his feet and said she would willingly follow him the rest of her life.

Jesus paid the ultimate price, by sacrificing His life, to free each of us from being enslaved by sin. Out of love and gratitude we should willingly serve Him with our lives.

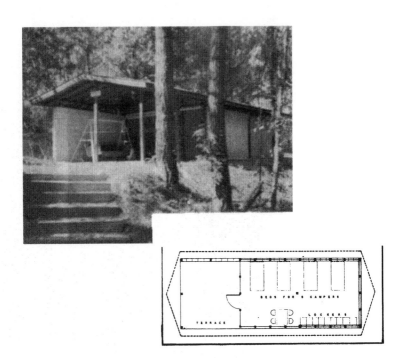

Cabin (From the 1956 Camp Westminster Brochure)

Buildings

O Beulah Land, sweet Beulah Land,
As on the highest mount I stand,
I look away across the sea,
Where mansions are prepared for me,
And view the shining glory shore,
My heaven my home forevermore

Wonderful grace of Jesus, Reaching the most defiled,
By its transforming power, Making him God's dear
child,
Purchasing peace and heaven, for all eternity;
And the wonderful grace of Jesus reaches me.

WHEN I ARRIVED at camp my second summer I found the new dining hall next to the Ad building.

The dining hall was a long building large enough to accommodate all the campers and staff at once, probably up to 150 or 200 people. Along the outside west wall were much-needed girls' and boys' rest rooms. Inside, near the door, was an old piano. In the back was an apartment, living quarters for the cooks, behind the large kitchen which had a walk in refrigerator/freezer and a huge conveyor type dishwasher.

The work crew guys spent hours dunking, scraping

and spraying each other, and the dishes before sending them through the steaming monster. It was really hot work for a summer afternoon in Georgia!

Ad Building and Dining Hall (1966)

Many yummy things were kept in the walk-in refrigerator. I believe the door was green . . . it was often raided by the junior staff at night . . . fruit, leftovers, desserts . . .

One summer I was assigned to help in the kitchen. The cooks had homemade rolls every meal. They kneaded the dough, let it rise, kneaded it again and shaped it into rolls which were placed on large flat metal pans on the counter to rise in the hot kitchen. The smell of fresh yeast rolls still takes me back to that kitchen. . . . As I helped make salad or dessert (banana pudding was the best), or set the table I would munch rolls as I worked. I gained about twenty pounds that summer. It might have been the only time I had fat on my skinny bones.

Oh, and as we worked we sang popular songs of the summer at the top of our lungs . . . "Moon River" . . . "Maria" . . . "Summertime" . . . We knew all the words but were not always on key . . . at least I wasn't!

Every Sunday evening we had an old fashioned hymn sing, "Singspiration." We would grab the chairs from around the tables and crowd up to the old piano in the back of the dining hall. Bruce and later Mary would play anything we asked for. We sang for an hour all the old favorite hymns at the top of our lungs . . . "And Can It Be" . . . "Great Is Thy Faithfulness" . . . . with "Beulah Land" and "When the Roll Is Called Up Yonder" . . . thrown in for fun.

Each week day after we got dressed we spent time near our cabin in private devotions which included learning the Bible verse for the day. When the bell by the Tabernacle rang, we would all gather by the flag pole outside the Ad building lined up by cabin, to watch the flag being raised and say the Pledge of Allegiance. (Sometimes someone's article of clothing would have to be lowered first!)

We had table assignments which switched every few days. The counselor at the head of our table would make sure we each knew our Bible verse for that day before we all said it together.

We ate family style and each camper was assigned a job of helping refill dishes in the kitchen, cleaning the table after the meal, or setting up beforehand.

During breakfast one of the girl counselors would lead devotions . . . a short thought for the day. Years later when I was a counselor and my turn came, I remember working long hours to prepare and having someone make illustrations for me. The talk had to do with a throne in your heart and who sat on the throne. Some of the possible throne sitters were sins in one's life, each illustrated as an ugly toad or snake or some other slimy creature. The object was to allow Jesus to stay on the throne.

The head table was located between the door to the kitchen and the side door leading back outside and over to the Ad building. The director, assistant director, their families, the hostess and sometimes Dr. Richardson and guests sat there. It was from there that any important announcements were made.

The most memorable singing in the dining hall was at lunch. Tables would sing to one or more campers or staff . . . "Round the dining hall you must go, Pete and Judy . . ." "Have you ever seen a kitchen sink, a kitchen sink, a kitchen sink, now you tell us one . . ." Some of them became a little crude. "Play Show" was stopped too, as it was not polite to open your mouth while eating. I really think Charles was getting tired of being called upon so often. "Sing us a song (name a person) sing us a song . . ." was a real favorite. Nancy and I were called on often to sing "We are crazy, we are crazy, we are nuts, we are nuts. Happy little morons, happy little morons, bla bla bla, bla bla bla" (wiggling fingers over lips while singing the bla bla bla part). And Knox was known for "The Midnight Special" and "Rock Island Line."

The "Midnight Special" became the name of the old enclosed van type truck used by the work crew to haul stuff around the camp grounds. Four of us on the staff used it EARLY one morning to drive to Stone Mountain, long before it was built up, and climb to the top to watch the sun rise. We had to leave camp about 3:00 am.

Lunch was also remembered for mail call. Each letter was examined, smelled, the outside read, guesses made about the sender and the contents before the camper to whom it was sent was called up to collect it. Love letters to staff members were made especially embarrassing. Care packages were a big deal and campers were expected to share with their cabin.

Postcards were positively wonderful! Every word was read with all possible inflection and innuendo. The summer after I graduated from high school my family did not want me to stay at camp on staff for the whole summer. I was devastated but entertained myself at home making up postcards to send to all my friends and imagining what mail call must have been like for them.

Although I never went hungry and liked the food, the only things now, fifty years later, that I can remember eating were rolls, banana pudding, canned green beans, scrambled eggs, and Kool Aid.

Oh yes, every Sunday afternoon we had a hot dog cookout down by the lake.

A Campwide Activity by the Lake (1966)

One of my other favorite buildings was the candy store. The new store was west of the Ad building near the parking lot. It had a waiting area in front of the long counter. Behind the counter were a cooler for cokes, a freezer for popsicles where we froze Milky Way candy bars. And lots of candy, chips and other goodies as well as books and T-shirts and sweatshirts. toothpaste, sun lotion, shampoo and whatever you might have forgotten to bring to camp. The summer I was assigned to work in the dining hall, eating rolls, I was also assigned to work in the candy store where I ate more than my share of Milky Ways . . . frozen of course.

I wish I still had my Camp Westminster sweatshirt! I do have a book, *Romans*, coauthored by Knox and Dr. Richardson, and a copy of *Reformed Doctrine of Predestination* which Charles gave me as well as several different translations of the Bible, all from the camp store. I also have a copy of one of the Tabernacle hymnbooks.

The Ad building was a favorite with counselors. We would use any excuse to spend time in the air conditioned lobby. The counselors met in the lobby during rest time most afternoons while the junior counselors were in the cabins. It was a time during which we shared our concerns about camp, problems with schedules, individual camper's needs, and planned upcoming events.

We also spent part of our time together praying for each other and campers. That was a very special time during which we would pray sentence prayers as we felt led to pray. Often someone came to the door or the phone rang . . . we just kept our conversation with God going on while someone from the group took care of the need at the door. I learned how real and relevant prayer can be.

There were two small offices off the Ad building lobby. One was the director's office which had a desk and phone, several bookshelves, chairs and a fan to blow the cold air conditioned air into the office. One day as Charles was reaching down to get something he had dropped, he cut his finger in the fan. Those were the days before safety fans.

The phone in the director's office was our link with the outside world. It was used to order supplies, call the doctor or parents and arrange transportation. I remember several times I used the phone to make plans to see Nancy, who had moved to Decatur. Sometimes I would get messages sent to me in my cabin to be in the office at a particular time in order to receive a call either from my parents, or to arrange to go on a date.

During my last summer at camp I became engaged while away for a weekend break. Poor Larry—every time he tried to call and leave a message about a time I could answer the phone, Charles would cross examine him to make sure he was "good enough for you." Since it was Charles who married us six months later, I think that was a form of marriage counseling!

The other office was the counselor's office, which contained a long table and several chairs along with a few books. That was a place to study and prepare Bible lessons, devotions, and sermons. We really respected each other's need for quiet to study.

In the back of the Ad building was the craft room, containing several picnic tables and scattered with all kinds of material like lanyard gimp, baby food jars for bank making, and other craft supplies. Sometimes we would sit on picnic tables in the craft room and sing. Charles would play the guitar and we would all take turns scratching each other's backs.

There was a guest room in the back of the Ad building. Back there were also two bedrooms with a small bathroom in each separated by a small kitchen. That was the infirmary . . . one room for boys and one for girls. The summer between eighth and ninth grade when I realized I was old enough to be on junior staff I begged the director, Knox, to let me stay for the rest of the summer. I remember saying I would stay and work for no pay and I "would even scrub the infirmary with a tooth brush and ammonia every day!" I ended up staying and I did a lot of cleaning but I don't remember scrubbing anything with a tooth brush. I was shuttled around from cabin to cabin wherever there was an extra bed. I don't remember ever being sick and having to stay in the infirmary but I do remember visiting several people who were sick.

Later buildings were the guest house not far from the parking lot where Charles the director and his family lived the last few summers I was at camp.

The last new building during the years I was there was the Dorm. It was on the road to the lake after you pass the back side of the Tabernacle, just beyond the old caretaker's cabin. It was originally built to be used during Family Bible Conferences held the last week of the summer when guest speakers came and families spent a week at camp together. The Dorm had a central lobby with two wings which each had several rooms with a bath between each two rooms. The number of girl campers grew some summers so that each wing was used as a cabin. I was glad I never had to live in the Dorm. It just didn't seem like camp.

At the very beginning of the summer the staff arrived a week early to prepare. Part of the preparation included the director meeting with the senior staff several times a day to plan the activities, schedule of events for the whole session as well as each day, and counselor assignments such as who would teach archery, softball, and crafts. The director also taught the Bible lesson to the counselors that they were to teach at cabin Bible study time.

Ball Game (1966)

The junior staff and work crew spent much of the time cleaning the camp after its not being used all winter. It was hot and we enjoyed each other's company much more than the work. Dr. Richardson would come along and check on us. Once he told a group of guys, "while you are resting why don't you move that pile of dirt from here to there?"

Ball Game (1966)

One day a group of us were assigned to clean the windows of the Dorm. There were dust and spiders inside and very high weeds next to the walls on the outside. I was cleaning with the inside crew. I don't remember who else was there that day besides Jimmy, Joey, Wayne and me, who were in one room together. We had a bucket of water and lots of newspapers. We were told to wash the windows and then dry them with newspapers which would get rid of all the dirt and streaks. I think that was Charles's bright idea.

We weren't your ordinary teenagers. We weren't

even singing that day. We were having a very heated theological discussion about predestination. The three guys, who would later each become Presbyterian ministers, were very upset at me for questioning predestination because it sounded so unfair. They locked me in the room with them and wouldn't let me out until I agreed with them. I remember throwing sloppy wet rags at them and saying, "You can't MAKE someone believe something." They finally let me go that day. Many years later I came to understand the great paradox of predestination.

Yes, predestination may seem "unfair" because we should all go to Hell, but God in His grace allows some of us to be saved. When you get to the door of salvation, on the outside it says "whosoever will may come" and once you are saved and Jesus has led you through the door and you look back, over the inside of the door it says, "you have not chosen me but I have chosen you"! That is the greatest paradox of Scripture!!!

Pool and Lake

Forbid it, Lord, that I should boast,
Save in the death of Christ, my God;
All the vain things that charm me most,
I sacrifice them to His blood.

Were the whole realm of nature mine,
That were a present far too small;
Love so amazing, so divine,
Demands my soul, my life, my all.

THE POOL, WHICH was Olympic-sized and spring-
fed, was new my first year at camp. It was just down
the hill from the girls' cabins, about halfway to the
lake. (I understand that the year before the pool
was built, the campers hiked to Lake Rockaway
for a swim, or rode in the Midnight Special truck.)
The water was my favorite part of camp. Almost the
whole time I was at camp I was either a camper in
the lifeguard's cabin or, as a counselor, I was the
lifeguard.

I became a certified lifeguard at camp by taking
the very rigorous course taught by India. There
were both instruction times, and swimming laps for
building endurance. For the final exam I was to be
in the water with several other counselors. One of
them would suddenly pretend to be in trouble and

I had to recognize the problem, "save" the person, and get him out of the pool safely. If anyone got into real trouble during the exam we were to pinch the other person to stop. I was a pretty small person 5'5" and less than 100 pounds. I was determined not to have to pinch my way out.

Pool (1966)

While we were all in the water, slowly Laurie, one of the bigger guys who was a lifeguard, began to sink to the bottom and stayed there. I had to dive to the bottom of the deep end, get his limp body up, carry him to the pool side and get him out. I don't think India thought I could do it but I did a nice job and saved Laurie. That opened the door for me to become the lifeguard several years later.

One of the special treats about being in the lifeguard's cabin was getting to go skinny dipping by moonlight. I think those were the only times I have seen ten girls having a wonderful time totally silent. We couldn't let anyone know, not the other girls' cabins because they would be jealous and not the boys' cabins because they would run through the woods to see what was happening.

I only remember having to "save" one camper. One summer someone invented the game "capture the watermelon." There were two teams in the pool with a watermelon (they float) covered with Crisco. During the mayhem of people trying to grab the giant fruit, one little girl went under and had no place to come up. She was fine after I blew the whistle to stop the game and grabbed her off the bottom. She needed a little rest on the side, that was all.

Speaking of almost drowning, I got pulled out one summer by worried Wayne. Each summer the camp was divided into four teams for the various activities. One activity was a swim meet with odd dives and strange strokes. I was very good at holding my breath for long periods of time under water. One event was to see who could swim the farthest under water. I dived in, swam the length of the Olympic-sized pool, turned, swam back, kicked off and was on my third length, all in one breath, when suddenly someone was pulling my hair! I was almost half way back. I had reached the spot where you could just stand up, when Wayne, along with many others, got very nervous and he jumped in to pull me out. I was afraid he had ruined my chances of winning, but I had already won by yards!

When we weren't in the water we were sunbathing by the pool or lake. One year we girls all got our first two-piece bathing suits. Mine was light blue and Nancy had a red and white polka dot one. She was a little nervous about wearing it so she covered up in a white eyelet beach jacket. Later that afternoon, when we returned to the cabin to change, we discovered she had little sun-burned red flowers on her midriff!

Water sports were not only at the pool but also at the lake. We learned all the canoeing skills including how to right a swamped canoe, and bobbing a canoe in order to move it forward when you have lost a paddle. Those lessons meant we ended up *in* the lake water. No one wanted to touch the bottom of the lake. Who knew what lurked in that slime? The canoes were also used for late night frog gigging, hiding counselors for counselor hunt night, and for dates.

Some of the counselors were dating each other; some of those were married later. Others of us would go on a date over the weekend break or have a date come visit camp. The perfect romantic place to be alone was in a canoe by moonlight.

The lake was a special place for two other reasons. Every Sunday afternoon we would go for a long walk (there was no swimming on Sunday) and return to the lakeside for a hot dog roast picnic.

It was a relaxed time during which we could just visit and eat.

The Lake (1966)

That same area was used the last night of each camp session for the big campfire. That was a solemn occasion where we gathered to sing hymns and listen to testimonies. Each camper had the opportunity to stand up holding a pine cone that he/she had picked up from a nearby pine cone pile, and tell what he had learned, how he had changed and how God had made a difference in his life that two weeks. When he was through speaking, he would toss his pine cone into the fire to symbolize letting his/her light shine for Christ. There were many tears those nights not only because of what was said but because camp had come to an end for another summer.

Activities

Hear Him ye deaf, His praise, ye dumb,
Your loosened tongues employ;
Ye blind, behold your Savior come;
And leap ye lame for joy.

CLOTHES WERE IMPORTANT and we tried to look nice, at least the girls did. Many of the boys had no sense of style or were overly conscientious about how they looked. One of the boy counselors who drove to camp filled his back seat, on a special clothes bar, with neatly pressed cotton shirts.

One summer it was popular to wear navy Bermuda shorts (never really short shorts) and a yellow checked shirt. The girls often wore white cotton sleeveless button down the front with a collar shirts. I remember such a white cotton shirt with a pink flower appliquéd on the back that I wore with gray shorts. I don't remember that we wore tee-shirts much at all.

Some of the girls loved to get sports tee-shirts or jerseys from the guys to sleep in at night. I had a high school football jersey from Mississippi in 1963. I think I "stole" it from Wayne for the summer.

Back then the only girls' tennis shoes were white canvas Keds which were supposed to be washable. Because of the red Georgia clay our shoes turned a yucky dirty orange. It was especially bad after a rain storm. One place that was terrible was the road to the lake beyond the caretaker's cottage. This road was a hill and when it rained the clay turned to orange liquid that oozed down the hill. In other areas of camp the rain turned the clay into slimy puddles. We used to wait until our shoes dried to knock off the dry mud. Washing did no good so we would polish them with liquid white shoe polish made for leather shoes.

Some of the Staff of 1963

There were both formal and informal activities. Sneaking out at night to go for walks and watch the stars was a favorite. There was an area outside behind the Tabernacle which had an old couch and a pingpong table. We never played the game but used to love to sit there and talk.

There was a trail that went off the southwest corner of the parking lot which "no one knew about". We would follow it through the woods to a little spring. If we were really daring, and some of the guys were (Wayne and Joey?), one could go even further to the watermelon farm and snitch a melon or two. I think that is where the melons came from the night the girls were terrorized by the giant green teeth monster.

When we signed up to play softball, we often just sat in the shade in a "back scratching circle" invented by Charles. Some of the guys would climb over the fence behind home plate into the nearby apple orchard and eat green apples which made them sick.

Most of the activities were attended daily, several in the morning and several in the afternoon. We would sign up ahead of time and take turns going to activities like crafts, archery, swimming lessons, canoeing, and softball. There was a tennis court, built about my third year at camp, but I don't remember anyone playing; maybe some of the boy counselors did. Long after my years, the camp started the horseback riding and a ropes program.

Each evening there was an activity in which the whole camp participated. Sometimes we went for a night swim or the counselors put on a fair for the campers.

Some evenings we divided the camp into four large groups and had a treasure hunt or counselor hunt, competing against each other. The prize was almost always a watermelon. I remember once as a camper finding a counselor in the middle of the lake in the bottom of a canoe but I couldn't reach him to tag him. Another year when I was a junior counselor, Laura, one of the guys and I hid beyond the lake under (inside) a blackberry patch. We spent the whole time eating blackberries and laughing. We never got caught.

Tennis Courts (1966)

We had swimming events in which teams competed in swimming and diving. We invented some pretty strange dives and swam great distances under water. At the "Olympics" on the softball field there were a number of odd track-and-field events. One I especially remember was crawling across the softball field while drinking YooHoo (yucky chocolate milk) through a baby bottle nipple. I think I still have scars on my knees from that race. We often had giant softball series. I was a shortstop for our team and could hit okay too.

Track Meet: Egg Throw! (1966)

Some summers we had a camp fair in the parking lot which consisted of booths with many kinds of games of skill. I can still see Jimmy dressed as a clown directing campers around to the various activities.

One activity was "Tacky Day" when we were each to dress in the worst combination of clothes we could come up with. A group of counselors acted as judges and picked the winner at lunch. One year the boy who won wasn't even trying to play. He dressed that way every day!

Future Camp Director Jimmy McGuire as Fair Gypsy (1966)

Each camp session we had Skit Night or Talent Night. One year our cabin made a soap opera story about fruit. One line went something like "Oh marry me, honey do . . . I wish I could but we can't elope . . . " Another year our cabin skits were all about Roman myths. My part was the boatman over the river Styx because my name is Karen . . . type casting ("Charon" is pronounced like my name)!

Camp Fair (1966)

I will never forget several skits on Talent Night. One was about a young soldier and a nurse on the battle field, both characters played by the same person. The soldier wearing an army hat was groaning and thrashing around as he lay dying. He quickly sat up leaning over where he had been lying and became the nurse holding a nurse's hat on his head. She asked him how she could help. She asked him what his name was so she could tell his mother he had died bravely on the battlefield. The actor quickly switched back to the army-hatted soldier groaning again and back to the nurse wearing a white hat asking him his name. This went back and forth a number of times in a very overly dramatic way. The last time the nurse begs him "Please tell me your name so I can tell your mother." Switching quickly, the soldier, with his last dying breath says, "My, my mother knows my name!" and he dramatically dies.

Another skit was a man crawling across the desert dying of thirst, very dramatic, saying, "Water, water, please I need water, water!!!" After slowly and dramatically crawling all the way across the stage, calling for water the whole time while dramatically dying he finally reaches a small pool of water (a dish pan) and totally changes to a happy faced boy, sits up takes a comb out of his pocket and wets it before combing his hair!

The most memorable skit was Jimmy telling the story, "Alice was my dog and *he* had fleas". Jimmy cried very hard the whole time he was telling the story. "Alice, he had fleas and I tried to get rid of them. Sob Sob. First I washed him and washed him but Alice, he still had fleas. Sob Sob. Then I brushed him and brushed him but Alice he still had fleas. Sob Sob. I tried picking them off, Sob Sob, and then used flea powder, Sob Sob, but Alice he still had fleas. Nothing worked. Then I got some kerosene and poured it ALL over Alice but he still had fleas. Sob Sob. So I got a match, (loud crying) and I lit the kerosene, (more loud crying), there was this terrible explosion and smoke and fire, Sob Sob . . . (then very quiet for a few seconds). When it was all over there was just a pile of ashes and down in the ashes was one little flea that looked up at me and asked, "Where's Alice?"

Between skits there were commercials. One memorable one was for "Ella May Hair Care for the Hair." Several girls demonstrated how to straighten hair while talking about this product using VERY strong southern accents.

All of the silly fun and competition and activities were very important but there was an even more important serious side at camp.

The Bell That Kept Us On Schedule (1959)

Tabernacle

Long my imprisoned spirit lay fast bound
in sin and nature's night;
Thine eye diffused a quickening ray, I woke,
the dungeon flamed with light;
My chains fell off, my heart was free; I rose,
went forth and followed Thee.
Amazing love, how can it be that Thou my
God shouldst die for me.

THE TABERNACLE was a large rectangular building on top of the highest hill on the camp property, surrounded by beautiful tall loblolly pine trees. It had a cement floor and cinder block walls that were about three feet tall and then continued as screen walls up to the roof. The roof was corrugated metal and had an overhang on the sides so that it was cool and did not rain in. There were three screen doors, one on either side of the stage and one in the center of the back. The stage was wooden with a pulpit in the center, a piano stage left, and several chairs stage right. On the solid cement block wall behind the pulpit was a banner saying "If God be for us who can be against us?" Rows of wooden pews filled the front half of the tabernacle and the back was an open space. Outside on the other side of the wall on which the banner hung was an area with cement floor and roof which had no walls. That area contained an old couch, a pingpong table, and some chairs.

Immanuel Tabernacle (1966)

Just outside the back door of the Tabernacle was a large old church bell on a stand with a long rope. That bell called us to activities, meals, and kept us on schedule all day. The first year I was at camp, when J.J. Scott was the director, he slept in a pup tent on the hill between the Tabernacle and the caretaker's house. Each morning he would play reveille to wake us up and taps in the evening to put us to sleep.

Although the Tabernacle was built for times of

worship, it was used for indoor games on rainy days. All the wooden pews were in the front half of the tabernacle so the large space in the back half could be used for indoor kick ball, or relay races. The cheers from the inside and the rain on the roof made it very loud.

In the Tabernacle was where we thought about the greatest questions of life. We sang hundreds of hymns and choruses which taught us the great truths of theology. First Bruce, then years later Mary accompanied us. Sometimes there were solos, duets or quartets . . . "How Great Thou Art," "God Giveth More Grace," "So Send I You," and "Day by Day" were just of few of the favorite special numbers I remember.

When it rained on the metal roof it made so much noise we had to out-sing the rain. "Showers of Blessing" was a favorite during those times.

The two hymns which bring back the clearest memories of sitting in the Tabernacle are "Great Is Thy Faithfulness" and "And Can It Be?" The fourth verse of "And Can It Be?" expressed clearly what happened to most of us who attended Camp Westminster. "Long my imprisoned spirit lay fast bound in sin and nature's night; Thine eye diffused a quickening ray, I woke, the dungeon flamed with light; My chains fell off, my heart was free; I rose, went forth, and followed Thee."

Our very serious Bible competitions between cabins were held in the afternoon in the Tabernacle. We memorized individual verses, long passages, and sometimes whole chapters of the Bible. That was not only very competitive but an important way to learn scripture. Back then we used the King James version. Today when I am reading from the NIV I sometimes stumble over the words because my brain wants to go back to what it remembers.

Dr. Richardson's Christian Economics course was taught there every afternoon just before supper. He would park his car down by the dining hall and walk up to the Tabernacle, stopping to talk to the campers as we all made our way through the screen doors. I can still hear his raspy voice explaining to us how to be responsible stewards.

Each evening a different boy counselor spoke telling a story, giving a sermon, or sharing a testimony. We were challenged to listen to God, accept Christ as our Savior, and live a life of service. Many, many campers and counselors became pastors, pastors' wives, missionaries, Sunday school teachers, and Christian leaders in academic fields.

Sometimes after vespers we would seek out a counselor to talk to about serious questions. I remember one rainy evening sitting in the back seat of a car with Charles, learning how to pray. "Whenever you think of someone you have not seen for a long time, that is God bringing that person to mind so you can pray for him or her." Throughout my life, as I have let my mind wander back to those years at camp, I have prayed for many, many campers and counselors I haven't seen for years.

One evening after Charles spoke no one seemed to respond. I remember talking to him out behind the Tabernacle referring to the book of Ephesians.

After we put on the whole armor of God we are to stand. Just stand, firm in the faith . . . in the Truth we have spoken. I discovered that night that I need to trust God through His Holy Spirit to use His Truth in others' lives. I may never know how the Holy Spirit has worked in another person's life and I don't need to know . . . that is up to God . . . I only need to faithfully speak Truth.

Tabernacle (1959)

My Very Last Night at Camp

I'd stay in the garden with Him though the
night around me be falling,
But He bids me go; through the voice of woe,
His voice to me is calling.
And He walks with me, and He talks with me,
And He tells me I am His own,
And the joy we share as we tarry there, None
other has ever known.

MY LAST NIGHT at camp was in August of 1966. As
had been my habit for all those years I wandered
around camp by myself in the dark looking up at
the stars and recalling so many wonderful memories. I ended up sitting in the front pew on the right
side of the Tabernacle. I could not believe this was
the end. Each summer when I left camp on the
last day I had cried very hard. Several summers
Charles had laughed and offered me a towel for my
tears! I was crying as I sat there, knowing this part
of my life was over. Quietly the door opened and
Charles walked in with flashlight in hand, making
his director-of-camp rounds, checking camp before
going to bed. We sat quietly for awhile, we talked,
and prayed. That is my last very precious memory
of camp. I honestly don't remember the next day
leaving camp and returning home . . .

Orlando Junior High Age Bible Study Group (1966)

The Orlando Connection

IN THE MID 2000's, about fifty years after Dr. Richardson's dream of starting Camp Westminster, there was an anniversary celebration at Westminster Presbyterian Church in Atlanta. J. J. Scott, the first camp director, shared some of his experiences and what camp meant to him. Others sent e-mails and letters sharing early memories and how camp had personally changed or formed their lives. This sparked a renewed interest in Camp among the old timers. An alumni magazine was published and ways to raise funds for clean up, revitalization, and scholarships were discussed during the next few years.

When I was a camper I was aware that other campers came from all over the South. Many came from the Atlanta area, children who were connected with Westminster Church. Others came from a church in Jackson, MS and the surrounding area, some from places like Tuscumbia AL, and Florence SC. There were groups of kids from churches all over the south whose pastors were friends of Dr. Richardson. News about camp spread by word of mouth. Friends brought friends.

During the time of renewed interest in camp in about 2007 I was asked if I knew the "Orlando connection" to camp. Starting in the late 1960's and throughout the 1970's busses from Orlando would arrive outside the Ad building each summer and unload excited campers. I never knew people wondered about how children from Orlando started coming to camp ... *I* was the Orlando connection!

When my Mama decided to send me and my brother to camp it was because she knew Dr. Richardson. She had grown up in Atlanta. After she became a young widow and single mother she moved back to Atlanta and lived with a friend. During that time she attended Westminster Presbyterian Church and became a Christian. She was aware of Dr. Richardson's dream and the purchase of property in Conyers for the camp. The year after she and my father were married was my first summer at camp. I loved it! I couldn't wait to go back the next summer. That next summer, 1959, I was the only person from Orlando. In 1960 I talked my friend Nancy into coming with me. Later several of the younger children in our church, including my little brother and sister, wanted to go to camp. The children, mostly girls, of friends from a Bible study group to which my Mama belonged began to attend camp. Soon their brothers wanted to go, too. My little brother and several of his friends attended camp, joined the work crew, and became counselors. The two summers I was a counselor Linda, who was also from Orlando, was my junior counselor.

My last summer at camp, during the junior high session, all the girls in my cabin were from Orlando. That summer I got engaged to be married at Christmas. Charles, the director, was coming to Orlando to officiate at my wedding. Back in

Orlando in the Fall I led a weekly Bible study for all the girls who had been at camp that summer. We had sleep-overs, parties, and they had a bridal shower for me before I got married.

Although 1966 was my last summer at camp there were bus loads of Orlando kids still going to camp for many years afterward. Does anyone from Orlando still attend camp?

I have been back to visit Camp Westminster three times since then. Once in the summer of 1970, on our way home to NJ from a visit in Orlando, my husband and I stopped to see Dr. Richardson. I remember sitting on his back porch on a hot June day, nursing my two month old son and talking about how camp was growing. In 1993, again on a return trip from Orlando, my husband and two youngest children and I, spent part of a day walking around camp as I told them about my experiences there. And, just this last fall in 2013 on the very cold day before Thanksgiving, my husband and I wandered around camp by ourselves looking at all the changes as I pointed out to him all that was still the same although fifty five years had gone by since my first day at camp.

Dr. John R. Richardson
(From the 1960 Camp Westminster Brochure)

Dr. Richardson's Dream

Ever lift Thy face upon me,
*   as I work and wait for Thee;*
Resting 'neath Thy smile,
*   Lord Jesus, earth's dark shadows flee.*
Brightness of my Father's glory,
*   sunshine of my Father's face,*
Keep me ever trusting, resting,
*   fill me with Thy grace.*

Dr. Richardson's dream of making a Christian Camp came into being as God led many people to become involved in creating Camp Westminster in the 1950s. Not only did he teach Christian Economics every afternoon, but he took a special interest in each member of the staff. He spurred us on with his amazing work ethic, praised and encouraged us. Once he sent a young homesick girl in junior camp to talk to me. He had heard me say earlier that I was "homesick for camp" when I was at home during the school year. He was sure I could "cure" that little homesick girl . . . I am still homesick for Camp!

Dr. Richardson often visited camp and, after several years, moved to a new home across Lake Rockaway Road from Camp. He had several horses there long before the Camp had horses, a barn and a riding program. It was his custom to go for a ride on his favorite horse all around the camp roads almost every day.

One day I was walking up from the girls' cabins to the Ad building. I was by myself. It was very, very hot and I had my hair tied back in a ponytail with a red ribbon to match my red checked shirt. I had on my favorite gray shorts. When I was in front of the dining hall I heard a noise and turned to see Dr. Richardson riding up behind me on a huge chestnut horse. He asked me to stand on the picnic table under the shady old loblolly pine trees. From there he pulled me up behind him and instructed me to hold on tight. I don't remember ever having been on a horse before. I wrapped my arms around his waist and leaned against his back. We galloped at full speed down those red Georgia clay roads, past the Tabernacle, along the girls' cabins, around the lake, into the woods, through the boys cabin area, and past the tree hit by lightning so long ago. I could feel the power and strength of the horse under me. I could not see ahead of me and was afraid to look, but I trusted Dr. Richardson and held on for dear life. After a long exhilarating ride we returned to the quiet picnic tables in the soft pine shade where he gently put me down. My heart was racing and I was smiling from ear to ear. I had lost my hair ribbon and I was tired.

But, I learned a wonderful lesson. Accepting Christ is like getting on the back of a powerful horse for a long wild ride . . . your whole life. You can't always see where you are going but you can feel power and control as you charge forward. With your arms wrapped tightly around the Truth of Jesus and holding on to your faith, you don't need to see ahead or fear anything. And, in the end, happy and excited, you are gently put down in a cool shady spot to rest.

I believe the streets of heaven are paved with red Georgia clay, shaded by tall loblolly pine trees whose sweet fragrance fills the air.

Acknowledgements

I am thankful for Knox Chamblain who proofread my earliest copy of this little book and made helpful comments and corrections just months before his death. He was the first person I met on my first day at camp, and years later was one of my favorite professors in seminary.

I am thankful for Charles Dunahoo who also proofread an early copy of this camp book. He has been a friend, mentor, and brother in Christ since my second year at camp. He even officiated at my wedding on his own anniversary nearly 50 years ago.

I am thankful for Wayne Herring for saying, "You should write a book about camp." He has been a brother, giving me great encouragement and helpful suggestions not only about this book, but about life over the past 57 years.

And, I am very thankful for my son Charles King who has held my hand encouraging and teaching me throughout this process. He made my little book come into being.

Made in the USA
Columbia, SC
19 August 2020